Workbook

Kerry Monroe

Acknowledgement

In the way a pearl of considerable value is to be highly treasured, so too, the true rarity of a time-tested friendship. To enjoy a friend in the smooth effortless times of life is always so delightful, but when the endurance of a friendship is tested in the demanding and toilsome seasons of life, that in itself is something to behold in humble gratitude.

To be a friend is to be one who cares about the small details of your life, who checks in often (even if they are miles apart in distance). But, to be considered a safe friend, one who knows you deeply and completely when you allow your true inner soul to be exposed wide open is extraordinary. This friend accepts that they are not here to fix you, but with an empathetic, non-judgmental heart, stands trusting in God's provision that HE will see you through.

Laurie, you are that friend to me. Thank you for the years of this very gift. Thank you for riding the many waves with me. You stood by as each wave came rolling in and you stayed in it until I could see through it and then beyond it. Thank you for putting the extra polish on this workbook and for having a heart to see it completed, knowing the many lives that it would touch and be a part of each person's healing.

A special thank you to my children, who have encouraged, carried, humbled and taught me a broader view of love. I love you more than words could ever express.

CONTENTS

Introduction

Grief Recovery. Consider for a moment that recovery from grief is not only possible, but a promise the Lord invites each of us to claim. Therefore, whatever sorrow that is tucked away in your soul that you may perceive as immoveable; let me assist you in taking that required first step forward on this formidable inward journey.

I hope to prepare you for the labor intensive work that lies ahead. So, if this is not a suitable time, please put the workbook down until you can face that first step. If you pray for strength and a willing desire then God will meet you where you are. He will be The Helper you seek!

True, honest, authentic recovery will strip the majority of energy from you. It will come as a cost. Hence the reason many will never truly do the work and never truly heal from their wounds. But the cost to not fully navigate through the grief process is even more costly; as I will explain further in the workbook. What do you have to lose but that constant shadow of grief which dominates and grips every moment of your thoughts, feelings and your perception of life (as you know it NOW).   You were made for more!

Shall we take the plunge and release our tightly held story? Shall we grant our great God His redeeming power in order to have Him fashion it into HIS story?

Allow me to walk alongside you on your journey. You may have taken my workshop, *Sojourning Through Suffering*. If you have, you will notice these seven chapters follow the same pattern and coincide with the workshop but at a deeper, more personal level. Let's embark on this sacred healing journey with the Lover of your soul.

Enter in. Enter into the battle.

3

Chapter One

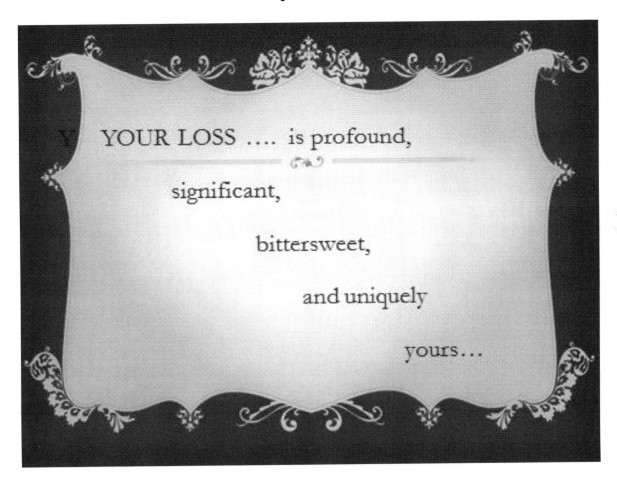

Y   YOUR LOSS .... is profound,

significant,

bittersweet,

and uniquely

yours...

Your Loss

As we move through this workbook, we will cover:
- The different types of losses and their impact on our emotions.
- What compound losses are.
- What tools are necessary to help maneuver through the grief process.
- What God's perspective is on it.
- That our pain should always be validated. Not to be misunderstood - I also believe in the continued healing accomplished through the Person of Jesus Christ. I believe healing **IN** His name, **BY** His name, **BECAUSE** of His name and **FOR** giving honor and glory to His name!

> "For from HIM and through HIM, and to HIM
> are all things. To Him be the glory. Amen."
> (Romans 11:36 NASB)

Simply put, we aren't taught how to grieve.

Encountering loss generates feelings of grief. Grief produces a "cry of the heart" that we have had to let something go. That *something* can be in the form of a person, place, situation or specific element that is dear to our lives.

💡 Name your loss(es):

_____

_____

_____

When you give voice to your losses by saying them out loud, and seeing them written down, it is one step forward in the healing process. Oftentimes, we have never thought about grief until we discover ourselves caught off guard and right in the middle of it! We may look to others to help in our time of need. However, they don't seem to really know how to walk alongside us or guide us on this journey. People often suggest that we hurry through it and just "get over it", which is not at all helpful.

💡 Have you experienced someone rushing you or suppressing any open dialog about your loss? Share how that made you feel.

_____

_____

_____

Let's debunk one of the biggest myths about grieving. It is said that, "Time alone heals all wounds." In fact, when "in grief" and looking ahead at nothing but time, the thought of facing our future not only seems daunting, but even excruciating. In comparison, facing time plus actively using the necessary tools (I will unpack this truth as we delve deeper into this workbook) for a healthy recovery, while also learning to surrender our pain into the waiting hands of God, we will personally witness how this equation moves us forward towards healing. Please be aware, healing not only takes time but varies between each individual.

💡 Have you found this statement about time healing all wounds to be true or not? Explain your response.

_____

_____

_____

When you have the ability, the capacity to breathe in the reality of this all-encompassing ache to see the enormity of the emptiness this loss has generated, and you see the effect it has brought, only then can God's Spirit swoop in and comfort you. He is waiting to do just that. Once you can fully face the bitter pain, He can and He will fully come so you can experience His healing.

Ask, in confidence and courage, for the faith to be sustained in this battle knowing that your faith rests in God's help. He also asks us to recognize and confront possible lifelong patterns which we've incorrectly used to deaden parts of our soul in controlling the pain.

💡 At this moment are you able to acknowledge some of the affects your sorrow has had on you personally? Please share it here.

_____

_____

_____

💡 How about the affects it has had on your family members and friends?

_____

_____

_____

💡 Ask yourself, "How committed am I to my own healing?"

_____

_____

_____

If the word "win" is associated with the concept of a winner, then you would assume the word "loss" is perceived with being a loser. No wonder we don't want to be forthcoming when speaking freely about our losses! We live in an age where acknowledging a winner is the norm. To actually give vulnerability a voice about having losses doesn't seem very attractive in this "top dog" mentality. So, we conform and determine to do almost anything to run from our loss and self-protect and/or self-medicate as a method not to feel the affect loss has had on us. We wear the veiled mask of disguise.

💡 How do you see God in your hurt today?

_____

_____

_____

💡 Can you (will you) see Him healing it as you give Him the authority to enter into it?

_____

_____

_____

On the other hand, if you are bold enough to share your loss with others they seemly imagine that the "effects" that loss has had on you is taking too long for their comfort. They may express little patience. This comes as a result from the fact that they are uncomfortable with, or are unaware of the mysteries that God reveals in the darkness.

💡 Have you experienced a person trying to "fix" your problem or wanting you to "hurry up" and be like you were before the loss? Maybe they've given you jobs so you can focus on something instead of your loss. Does that make you feel more like a victim rather than a person who is honestly trying to authentically delve into their loss and the emotions wrapped around that loss? Share your thoughts about that.

_____

_____

_____

What would you like others to know that would help them understand your grief?

_____

_____

_____

I don't believe people realize how arrogant it is to think we know the reason behind why the effects of this loss have occurred. I am convinced there are those who are simply uncomfortable with not having answers in life. They want to wrap life up into a neat, tidy package, as if what's inside could/should have all the answers of why God allows suffering. How often are our perceptions of the "whys" incorrect? We live in a broken world and stuff happens. Certainly there are consequences for our choices, but the fact is life is messy. Be aware that it takes time (longer than you might realize) to untangle the emotions connected to your loss.

The root of many of our issues stems from wanting to take control ourselves in handling life's situations. It can be a weighty problem that we aren't even aware of. Emotions and feelings are wonderful. They let us know we are alive. That being said, we certainly want them to work for us and not against us by being controlled by them. If you find yourself in a hard place right now, you can bank on the fact that this feeling will not always be there. Emotions are like waves; they wash over us and then leave us.

"We take captive every thought to make it obedient to Christ." (2 Corinthians 10:5)

How can you apply that Bible verse on a daily basis?

_____

_____

_____

💡 Can you see how taking God's Word and applying it to our situations is being deliberate in our own healing process? Why?

_____

_____

_____

As a child of the Living God, a Christ follower, we can have the confidence to believe that as we learn to move out in His strength, allowing Him to draw out from us what He has already put into us we give Him honor by living our lives transparently. When we fight to regain control over the flood of emotions that wash over us from the loss, we must remind ourselves that Christ has already won this battle. We always step out *FROM* victory, never needing to grasp aimlessly for it. To proceed beyond where we now find ourselves using the right tools (which will be expanded on later), in a God-honoring way, we commit to adapt to the loss by assimilating it into our lives instead of having it be the all-consuming center of our lives.

💡 List any changes you have noticed when it comes to your relationship with Jesus since the loss.

_____

_____

_____

💡 Have you invited God into this ache? If you haven't, explain why.

_____

_____

_____

💡 How does inviting God into the ache of the loss look in reality?

_____

_____

_____

💡 Can you name the biggest change this loss brings for you spiritually?

_____

_____

_____

💡 Can you name the biggest changes for you relationally?

_____

_____

_____

Have you ever seen in the scriptures a "one-size-fits-all" timeline for grief? When you can see beyond today's ache and let God take your pain, He can use that one thing as a catalyst for helping others. This is how we are deeply known. THIS is the real, honest, intentional, relationship God wants to have with us. It is then that we can have deeper relationships with others as well.

A lot of questions are raised in this first chapter. I do this with a purpose. Before we can really break down the different types of losses and/or receive the helpful tools to assist us, I need you to be honest. Starting with a baseline of where you are at this moment in time in your grieving journey will help you to see the progress you've made.

So, whatever stage of loss you find yourself in, whether it is suffocatingly fresh, or a bit further along in the process; whether standing strong, or struggling for answers (perhaps you picked up this workbook to help a friend or loved one who is suffering), the purpose of our time together here is to intentionally and honestly embrace our grief head-on. Yes, to even dive into those dark, deep waters when necessary.

Above all . . . Pray to the One who knows you best.

Chapter Two

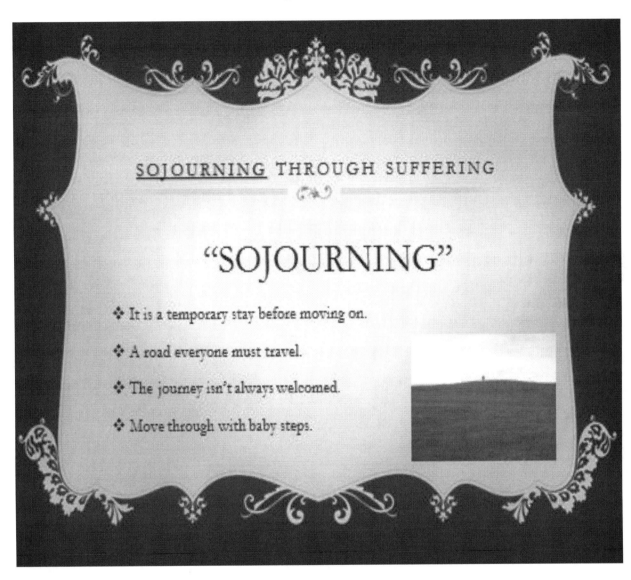

Sojourning Through

The definition of the word sojourn (verb) is: "to stay for a time in a place; live temporarily".
The definition of the word journey (verb) is: "a traveling from one place to another, usually taking a rather long time".

To decipher this with a finer understanding means that our season to travel through grief is not only temporary in duration, but it is also a much needed journey that will challenge and demand more time from us than what we first comprehended. You may feel as though you will be stuck dwelling in this place (this place of sorrow) forever because the pain is so acute, but with the help of the Holy Spirit, I assure you, you will move forward.

One of the ministering assignments of the Holy Spirit is to be our Helper. In the original language that the New Testament was written in, the word for help is 'sunantilambonotai'. I like how David Seamand's breaks up that big word to my level of understanding in his book, *Healing for Damaged Emotions*: "This is a combination of three words: Sun means "along with, together"; anti, "on the opposite side"; and *lambano*, "take hold of". When you put them together, *sunantilambonotai* means, "to take hold of together with us over on the other side."

Are you in need of getting out and getting to **that** other side? Will you be deliberate in the way you first see your need, and what might be hindering you from reaching the other side? When you see your need and ask for the Helper to work with you, then, and only then, can you begin accepting that you can't simply do this on your own?

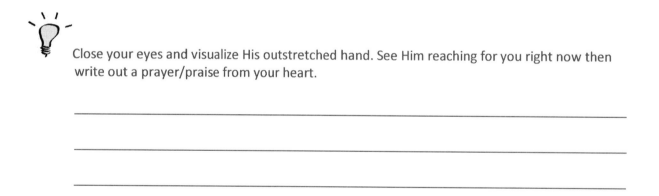

Close your eyes and visualize His outstretched hand. See Him reaching for you right now then write out a prayer/praise from your heart.

_____

_____

_____

You and you alone must take the responsibility to ask the Holy Spirit for the help. Write out your request to Him. See it boldly written in front of you; its okay that you may not truly be feeling or believing it yet. Sometimes we simply must declare it, in faith, and wait for our heart to catch up.

Allow me to divulge a very realistic picture for you, IF you haven't experience it yet yourself. When you enter into the arena of wrestling through your grief it's going to be difficult! Once the numbness, the shock, or even the indifference wears off, and you begin the undeniable work in healing, you will be better able to wrestle in and through the pain. The whys, the disappointments, the murky fog, the sadness, the black hole, and the anger at times can be compared to being held down by an invisible force of a whirlpool. You might find yourself flat on the floor, arms wailing, and crying out to the Lord in protest. That is okay. That is what real, raw emotions can look like and feel like. And that is why so many people just don't want to deal with their pain and seek other ways to shut it off. But, we are called to live by higher standards and face all parts of our emotions with a candid and sincere attitude.

Do you think our God is disgusted by the way we might be "working out our grief"; by what others might describe as a two year old type of tantrum? You can never disgust Him. He is your Father who comes to you with compassion. He sent His Son, Jesus our High Priest, who knows what real, raw emotions look like, sound like, but most of all feel like. The Holy Spirit will swoop in and meet you on the floor where you may find yourself in a puddle of tears. Let Him wipe your drippy nose, dry your tears and lovingly help you back up. As a comforting Helper, He will take you to the other side of the emotional outburst. So, don't be afraid, shocked, or embarrassed by it. It was probably much needed.

> "I am worn out from my groaning. All night long I flood my bed
> with weeping and drench my couch with tears." Psalm 6:6

Can you admit where you are? Have you experienced or heard someone minimize their own grief using cliché's like:

"Oh, my grief wasn't a piece of cake or a walk in the park, but I got through it". I am exceedingly more encouraged when someone quotes a meatier statement like, "I was in the dark night of my soul."

Or "I was called into the house of mourning yet the Lord was there. He was giving me the room and time to work it out in my own way. *Then* He brought me to the other side."

The work of grief not only takes energy and patience, but it often zaps all your concentration. It can be hard to formulate your thoughts and words clearly to others. This is frustrating but very normal. Your mind is swimming through muddy waters and foggy thinking can be exhausting. Give yourself grace. In stressful times, the central part of the brain, the hippocampus, responsible for memory is affected and actually shrinks. Also, our brain's neurons, which are responsible for problem-solving, coping with challenges, emotional processing, impulse control, and regulation of glucose, are affected too. When you are aware that your biological chemistry is changing because of what you have experience you can then learn to be more patient and gentle with yourself (or others).

When family and/or friends worry about you, let them know you only have enough energy (at this time) to work and process through your grief. When the process is further along, you will have the capacity and a better grip on being "present" in their lives.

This is also where it can get tricky. You might be isolating more than what is healthy. A loving, safe person who has been through their own grief process may recognize where you need to be challenged and confront (hopefully in love) the space you find yourself in. Of course, this is never easy to receive but it is good for us to take in wise council. It may be the very word you need to start moving forward.

Our pain can be all consuming and we can become highly self-focused without realizing it. So, knowing that, even knowing that all though your heart might not be truly "into it", you do need to start reinvesting and keeping those relationships viable by working on them.

Where, if at all, have some of your relationships been neglected?

_____

_____

_____

Would you be willing to commit now to start working on healing those relationships? What are some helpful ways you can begin doing that?

_____

_____

_____

When a crisis comes into our life, and they will, oftentimes we have a knee-jerk response of thinking negatively about the difficult interruption they generate. It's our natural bent to do this. Once we get our equilibrium back, and can feel our feet back on the ground (when life normalizes a bit more) we can look at these crisis events with a more positive attitude knowing they can be a turning point in our lives. Turning points are opportunities to grow; for a new way to approach life and possibly shake off bad habits or unhealthy coping mechanisms we've developed and have been hanging onto for years.

Can you name some good points that have emerged from this struggle?

_____

_____

_____

Would you be willing to observe any possible discrepancies between your own perception of reality and how God sees your reality? Remember that God's ways are not always our ways, or His timing.

_____

_____

_____

Every part of life is entwined with gains and losses. Let me give you two simple ways of how those two are intertwined so you are not easily caught off guard.

Example #1: Your child goes off to college. The **loss** might be an empty home or the dynamic of the siblings' roles changing. And, of course, you miss that child. The **gain** is that their independence is the very thing you have been working them towards all these years and they are on the cusp of starting life out on their own.

Example #2: A planned or unexpected move. The **loss** is that you miss the comfort of the home you're leaving, as well as friends who lived in close proximity. The loss can also be accompanied with uncomfortable feelings from being surrounded with unfamiliar places. The **gain** is moving into a new home with the chance to meet new friends, explore new places and make new memories.

Coming back and taking a look at your loss... If you are cautiously wondering how long this mourning takes, it actually depends on several factors:

- The intensity of the relationship in which you lost.
- Your ability to handle loss upon loss and how/if you've worked through losses in the past.
- There are also chronic types of losses to be aware of: being a survivor of a loved one who chose to die by suicide, battling mental illness, chronic pain, types of handicaps, and so on. We need to also acknowledge the grief that comes with some of the losses we carry from the past.

The many different types of losses will be thoroughly covered in Chapter Three, but here is a brief overview looking at the loss of an intimate person within the direct sphere of our relationships, or other special people in our lives.

- **Loss of a spouse** – the incredible ache caused by the loneliness of missing that life partner; the death of many dreams of growing old together.
- **Loss of a parent** - can stir feelings of being abandoned or orphaned.
- **Loss of a sibling** - this is the most neglected loss and not acknowledged as being significant.
- **Loss of a grandparent** - although more expected, one will feel the loss of history, unconditional love, and acceptance.
- **Loss of a child** - the most intense and debilitating loss. It is long lasting (when does a parent stop being a parent?). Death can never sever these bonds.

So, you may ask, "How long will the mourning last?" I don't know. Will you ever be the same again? No. Yet, you can live a broader, richer, fuller life despite the loss. The feelings you are now experiencing (anxiety, poor sleep, loss of appetite, even experiencing shallow breathing, loss of interest, intense crying, etc.) are the ramifications of your deep sense of loss.

But when the complexities of the emotions that loss can bring on begin to diminish, you will discover you're at a turning point! You will enter into a new phase and sense pleasure again! You will start noticing little joys in daily living and start making plans again.

However, if you choose not to do the hard work, despair will seep into every aspect of your life. The shadow of grief will follow you all your days. Apathy creeps in and you disconnect. Disinterest spreads and takes over. Your life, memories, and emotions become stunted and frozen by the "event". Apathy is the enemy to real, genuine healing and joy.

> Isaiah 43:2, 3, 5 (paraphrased) "When you go through deep water, I'll be there. When you go through rivers of difficulty, you won't drown. When you walk through fire of oppression, you won't burn."

Are you *there* now? In those deep waters, crossing the river of oppression, feeling the heat of a fire? Can you give your experience a voice? What would that voice sound like?

_____

_____

_____

What is the hardest part of this time for you? For those close to you?

_____

_____

_____

Would it help if you only *knew* when this grief would be over? Why? In what way would that help you?

_____

_____

_____

Take the time to formulate your thoughts and words. They are tools to aid and move you forward. It is much the same as physical therapy; helpful in the healing after an injury or surgery.

In order to push through a period of being stuck, do the "one thing". For you, if you find yourself in trauma or shock right after a crisis, your "one thing" might be to get up and brush your teeth for the day. Good for you. (One day at a time and one reasonable task at a time.) Then the next day you will be able to brush your teeth and take a shower. One day you will find yourself visiting with a trusted friend. Go slowly. Go purposefully. This is self-care. One step, one day at time with what works best for you.

BUT do push *through*! You must commit to being intentional. Be deliberate in your own healing. Pledge to face it down; don't turn off your emotional switch by wearing that old familiar mask; or keep things as "status quo" by sweeping what truly makes you alive under the rug! You will have to fight against those urges; fight against the inclination that others want you to "just bury it" and move on.

Time after time, in the hope to regulate and dull our emptiness, our endless wanting and pain, we inflict ourselves with coping mechanisms of self-medication. Consider all the myriad of ways we have intentionally, and even unconsciously, deadened our pain. We've tried to satisfy our longings, or handle our fears through therapeutic shopping, gorging on food, running around in busyness, thrill seeking, avid gambling, hiding behind the computer, getting caught up in the magnetic pull of social media, binge drinking, zoning out on drugs (legal, or not), spacing out in front of the TV, being a news junky, etc. The list goes on and on.

Instead of erecting substantial walls around the emptiness, we need to acknowledge we have the emptiness. We need to be present with the reality of how it feels. It will probably be uncomfortable. When we can recognize/accept our need, then we can be honest and hand it over to the Holy Spirt to take a grip of and replace it with God Himself. He will come in and infiltrate every nook and cranny of our soul. Our faith is in His work – it's not us having "faith" in faith. Jesus Christ is the object of our faith. He is our hope.

Our sincere, honest work comes when the head knowledge (of God, of faith) we've been accustomed to in an almost mechanical way, begins to drops 18" from our head and is driven down into the core of our heart (and is felt and understood in a more personal way). It shakes and awakens our reality. It calls upon the great strength that we receive from the Lord to fully taste the bitterness, the pain, the loss; prudently staying there to understand our desperate need for Him. THEN we can, and will, fully taste the sweet truth that God will stand in its place.

This is the GREAT EXCHANGE! He gives Himself for us to feast on and delight in. All other things are counterfeit to Him. He needs us to see that. He swoops down and sweeps in for us to swell with satisfaction. He wants to take our fears and turn them into a healthy curiosity of the future things He has planned for our lives. His desire is for you! His gaze is that of a Bridegroom with much longing.

We must remember that the Lord doesn't need to work in time, space, or dimension as we understand it. Release those man-made timetables. He penetrates forgotten areas and does the job of deep cleaning in our souls. Give Him the permission and the allotted time it takes for you and your personal journey through grief. Why did Jesus come? Was it not to break the invisible chains and snares? To come set the prisoner free? There are all kinds of jails. Not all have iron doors with locks that keep us captive or constrained.

> Isaiah 61:1 *"The Spirit of the Lord GOD is upon me, because the LORD has anointed me to bring good news to the afflicted; He has sent me to bind up the brokenhearted, to proclaim liberty to captives and freedom to prisoners"*

What are some of the ways you can see your own chains?

_____

_____

_____

What are some ways you can start taking care of yourself right now?

_____

_____

_____

Above all.....Pray to the One who knows you best.

22

Chapter Three

Suffering

It's quite the undertaking to wrap your thoughts around words like: pain, death, tragedy, suffering, crisis, heartache, and trial. How much more grueling it is when these events interrupt each of us personally. When events like these collide into our world (and they will) often our first reaction is to panic. You, and the world as you know it, are thrown off balance. Maybe your belief system has been temporarily tested, shattered.

Scripture instructs us not to be surprised by trials that seem to burst in and are delivered with a wrecking ball, and yet we always are surprised when it happens. *(1 Peter 4:12 "Dear friends, do not be surprised at the fiery ordeal that has come on you to test you, as though something strange were happening to you.)*

Maybe it seems more intense from having the affluence and comforts of living the American life, which has somewhat isolated us and made us believe that we are safe within an insulated bubble of protection. It's human nature to feel violated by the interruptions that clash into our 'status quo'. Or perhaps we feel violated and angry because our life pattern has had one difficulty after another, and now *this* has happened to us. Our hurts, doubts, anger, sadness, loneliness (you name it) threaten our understanding of how life *should* operate for us. Have we (you) been fooled by the illusion of control?

When were you first shocked by the realization you were not in control?

_____

_____

_____

Honestly, how uncomfortable does that make you feel?

_____

_____

_____

Being alive in this world guarantees that we will always be faced with having to resolve problems and one of them is having to learn to let go (say our goodbyes). I don't fully understand why we have not been better prepared for this inevitable truth. Instead, if we dare to be raw in our honesty (in the four corners of the inner most part of our heart), we often wonder why. Why does God allow suffering? Why didn't He answer my prayer in way I requested? Doesn't He care? Can He really be trusted? Is He even good? These are outrageous and shocking sentences and NOT what you might hear or have spoken out loud in the typical Christian community. But I have to wonder if you might not have had thoughts like these, possibly for a moment, after the landscape of your life was forever changed. Our God knows.

The Lord isn't asking us to be super plastic spiritual beings. He knows we have moments of lashing out. He isn't disappointed that these types of feelings come to us. And He isn't afraid of our temper. In time, our trust returns and we can once again focus on all the promises we've been given; we hold them anew. It's that darn "testing" that is problematic and challenging to us. We would be okay if we only knew how long we had to struggle through it. It would be easier on us if we had some kind of timetable; could see the end of our testing. That way we could put our head to the wind and plow through it. Yet, isn't this where *faith* comes in?

Have you discovered that God gives grace day by day? That the faith you need is not something you can gather ahead of time, but that you must cry out for it moment by moment?

_____

_____

_____

Have you found God faithful to His promise to give you the faith you need to carry on?

_____

_____

_____

Most of us are familiar with the James 1:2 *"Consider it pure joy, my brothers and sisters, whenever you face trials of many kinds"*. Joy in my suffering? How is that possible when the pain is so acute and overwhelming that there is only a throbbing ache that takes my very breath away? Or maybe for you, the numbness has set in and it has almost turned to apathy and it's hard to "feel" any joy (or much of anything)!

First off, joy does not mean minimizing our truth about the pain we are presently experiencing. *Joy* is the honest, deep-seated internal belief that somehow God will bring goodness from it (whether that be on this side of heaven or the other). *Joy* is being secure that we can give God glory from this time (if we allow it). Pain and joy go hand in hand. *Joy* knows we are becoming more like Christ through our suffering. *Joy* is surrendering the fact that even if we are not released from the pain of this world, we will forever be pain-free in heaven. *Joy* is the knowledge of where we are going and Who it is that loves us! "Happiness" is all about external situations, which constantly change. *Joy* is a deep-seated trust in God, who never changes.

God works the affairs of our heart out in hidden and concealed places. I often think of it as a "Winter Season" of the soul; a place and time where we must hunker down, where our breath and heart beat slow down to a deliberate rhythm. The winter season may not suggest growth as seen on the outside, but growth is taking place on the deepest level. It is reliable and proven. As one begins the season, you must enter the cave and be stripped of all self-sufficiency. There will be no multitasking in the cave time. Your primary job is to do the "one thing", work on grief. God speaks ever so clearly there. He will reveal Himself to you and will share with you the faith you need to move forward.

Share some of the ways it has been difficult to receive the faith and help God offers.

_____

_____

_____

What would be some steps to take to change that?

_____

_____

_____

We are not left alone in our battles. God originated faith, and He is the only avenue to faith, as well as being the One who funnels it into us. Our job in this is only to receive the faith He offers.

Your Loss
A loss means some kind of connection has been broken and now your life will be different. Let's take a moment to understand the ramifications of loss and the ripple effect (other losses that follow the primary loss).

Types of Losses:
This will be a broad overview exploring the many varieties of losses. Some you may not have even considered as a loss.

Relationship: Some type of bond has been broken; the "we" is now an "I". You might find changes in social interactions, or if it's within a group setting there can be a disruption/balance upset because the roles of each person within the family/group might now be played out differently and relationships shifted. This is called a "systemic" loss. There is a huge point of change within family dynamics when a death of a spouse/parent has taken place.

Impaired health (mental): A person may experience less independence and/or finances. Their world moves slower and becomes smaller and it becomes more difficult to maneuver outside in a fast paced world. The frustration is a loss of privacy when one must have a helper always nearby or in their home; especially if that person is not a member of the family). Bodily functions differ now and can cause embarrassment so the person no longer goes out in public. There could be loss of the ability to enjoy past hobbies, or to even afford them. Add to this the losses in the life of the caregiver which would include frustration, exhaustion and anger. A confusing new world opens up in trying to understand, acquire and deal with needed social services, multiple Dr. appointments and already confusing insurance claims.

Job: Income declines; identity struggles of who you are now without your job; stress from others that may be relying on you financially; possible future need to sell a home, car, belongings; relocation, or change of the kid's school. All these "maybes" can bring fear.

Dream: The way you dreamed of your future is now gone, shattered. Expectations crushed, hope's shaken, and that white picket fence isn't going to happen for you.

Identity: You might struggle with feelings of insecurity; the safety bubble has burst. Your good name might have been compromised; your credit score altered because of lost/stolen identity; fear can set in as well as the feelings of instability. There is a constant looking over your shoulder. You feel like a dark shadow is looming overhead.

Purity: You've made some bad choices or you've been violated in some way. Your good name is in question. Your trust is compromised. There is a threat of possible types of disease, some life threatening. Pregnancy can ensue, or because of disease there now won't be any pregnancies in your future.

Move: When a person moves from familiar surroundings, many comfortable landmarks will be missed. Those easy routes have been left behind. Relationships change and moving to new schools or new job can seem unpredictable, daunting and raise anxiety/stress levels.

Person: Beside the huge "impact" of losing a loved one, think about the secondary losses of not having this person in your life. You might be missing your protector, prayer partner, friend, handyman, tax preparer, mechanic, cook etc. You also might have to move, financial situations change, or a change in schools is in order. You might have lost your future grandchild, or there is no child now to carry on the family name, or to care for you when you age. Often today's losses become future losses.

Age: All of the above types of losses accumulate more frequently now and can seem more intense; more overwhelming.

Add to the mix of all the losses mentioned above and we now have:

Compound Loss: Unresolved childhood losses bring about complexity in dealing with grief. There is intensity to each loss from the frequency each loss carries.

Continual Loss: Comes when living with a handicap or acute illness, the aging process, or trying to understand a mental disorder.

Ambiguous Loss: Includes any kind of vague or hard to explain loss. Ambiguous losses can be some kind of loss that is not validated or socially recognized; such as miscarriages, infertility, adoption struggles, kidnappings, life changes of the caregiver, death with no physical body to mourn, guilt over an abortion, a prodigal child, the loss of a beloved pet, etc.

Conflicting Loss: Often when a family member commits a horrendous crime or is incarcerated, that loss can feel very conflicting; resulting in embarrassment, unresolved anger, or bitterness. Death by suicide or an overdose can also bring up conflicting feelings. These types of losses are often taboo subject matter and people (even surviving family members) will feel judged or under the shadow of stigma and shunning (whether real or imagined).

Threatened Loss: A spouse wants a divorce; add that the court appointments and you've now got compound issues added to that loss. Other threatened losses: a medical report with an unexpected diagnosis; investments that fluctuate; company downsizing, etc.

You might have experienced a variety of any of those losses mentioned above. Try to break each one down. Maybe journal or write a letter to see the possible ripple effects that have happened to you or to a family member. Once you see it in writing, be gentle with yourself. You are dealing with a lot!

Remember who you are *in* Christ and that your worth and future is in Him. Anything else that you get your identity from (i.e., job, spouse, health, etc.) cannot, and does not, define your worth. You get your identity from Christ (*1 Peter 2:9 But you are a chosen race, a royal priesthood, a holy nation, a people for his own possession, that you may proclaim he excellencies of him who called you out of darkness into his marvelous light.*) The losses that I mentioned are all potentially changeable and God never changes!!

> *Colossians 2:9-10 "Let us know we are complete in Christ and that in Christ all the fullness of the Deity has been given to Him."*

Keep that truth close to your heart. You need that reminder every so often.

Above all.....Pray to the One who knows you best.

Chapter Four

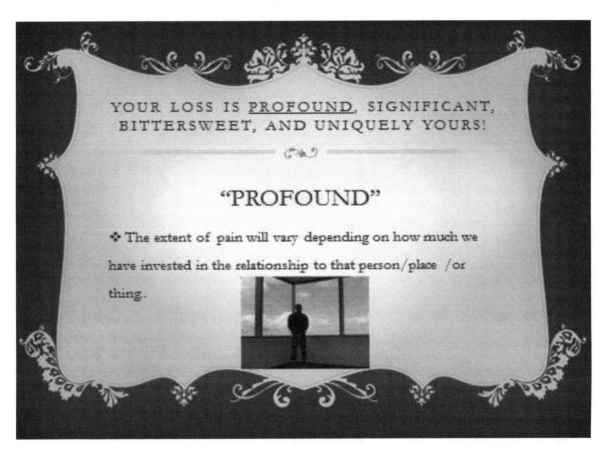

YOUR LOSS IS <u>PROFOUND</u>, SIGNIFICANT, BITTERSWEET, AND UNIQUELY YOURS!

"PROFOUND"

❖ The extent of pain will vary depending on how much we have invested in the relationship to that person/place /or thing.

Profound and Significant

Loss has been described as feeling like you're being covered with a heavy blanket or as a constant companion. A person might be going along their merry way and doing pretty well, then out of nowhere, grief crashes down like a violent wave, sucking them to the depths of the ocean floor, snatching their very breathe away.

Yes, your loss is profound.

As much as the fact that your loss is profound, we certainly don't want to minimize the impact in any way, shape, or form. You should also not have it loom out of proportion. You may ask, "When do I know it has ballooned out of portion?" and "When am I honestly dealing with the reality of my loss in the timely manner needed?" It's a delicate balance that I would liken to walking a tight rope. I would also say that it is not my place to tell you when that time is. One must walk closely with the Lord; His Holy Spirit is your guide. Everyone will journey differently, and within a different timetable. I would also say that it is not my place to tell you when that time is.

We are not one dimensional creatures on a screen or piece of paper. We have three dimensions: body, soul and spirit. Grief (reaction to loss) is multi-faceted. Reactions to individual losses will vary on how much has been invested with that person or thing.

Let's take a moment to see some actual physical symptoms the body can undergo with stress:

- Physical - Exhaustion, dry mouth, shortness of breath, tight throat, nausea, muscle tingling, diarrhea, change in eating habits, anxiety, sensitivity to sound, irritability, confusion, sleep disturbances, crazy thoughts, fleeting thoughts of death. Please note that it is very normal to have moments of wishing to die. However, if you begin to obsess, or start making plans, please call the ***Suicide Hotline: 1-800-273-8255***. Be very careful with repetitive thoughts of wishing to die which can begin a very dangerous pattern and cycle that becomes hard to stop and will amplify towards fruition.
- Cognitive - You start imagining danger is everywhere. You magnify the negative and over generalize. If you find yourself making comments like "always", "never", or the overused and not helpful "could of, would of, should of", you will want to stop yourself; change your thinking and speaking habits which lead to negativity. Behavioral changes that are harmful can start when you begin to avoid people, places, or things. Also watch out for self-defeating behaviors like cutting (self-mutilation) or self-medicating in seeking relief.
- Social – You are isolating yourself rather than going to events or leaving home. When you find yourself withdrawing, recall the allegory about the logs in the fireplace: As long as all the logs are closely gathered, then the fire roars. Warmth and light are generated. But for the log that slowly rolls to the side, its embers fade out.
- Spiritually – You find yourself moving further away from God and God's people, or church. It is easy to talk yourself out of many things. That is why God lifts our spirit towards His Word; to listen and to follow. It is how we apply His truth to our lives.

Be aware of some of these assorted symptoms. Bear in mind that we do not have to fear our truth. Candor and a sincere look into our present situation will help us to move forward. All of these can be "turning points" to go a different direction, if needed.

How far on the road to recovery are you? If you don't think you are very far, don't stress about it. Instead, use this as an opportunity to establish your baseline (a starting measurement to illustrate that you are moving forward). Don't be surprised, or hard on yourself, when you take a few steps back while moving forward in this process.

_____

_____

_____

This scripture bears repeating:

| "We take captive every thought to make it obedient to Christ." (2 Corinthians 10:5) |

As stated in the verse in 2 Corinthians 10:5, what thoughts do you need to take captive? How difficult is it for you to truly believe what God's Word reveals?

_____

_____

_____

What kind of "log" from the fireplace allegory are you today? How can you see that changing?

_____

_____

_____

"Significant"

Life has happened to you. You have a story to tell. Will you share your story? What part of *your* story can you identify with in the situations below?

**Please do not read through this list as though it were a grocery list. Take a moment. Pause after each sentence. Is this your truth? Could it be the truth of another? Spending time in the Valley of the Shadow of Death (whether it is our own, or that of a loved one) teaches us compassion.

What is your significant story?
- The echoing silence of a now empty house.
- The heart wrenching ache as you stare down into an unoccupied crib with your wanting and barren arms.
- The awkwardness at having to remove a familiar table setting (chair) at the kitchen table.
- One less stocking to put up this Christmas.
- The stark reminder every morning and evening that you can't escape when seeing/feeling that the other side of the bed is no longer occupied.
- The wedding ring that discreetly needs to be placed in a drawer.
- The underlying rage at the one who stole something from you.
- A body bruised or defiled in some way.
- Having to say goodbye to each room of your home because it isn't yours anymore.
- The addiction that has a mighty grasp and your battle in it only intensifies the want.
- No one to walk you down the aisle and give you away, or to carry on the family name.
- The obstacles, stigma and limitations you and your loved ones face; which others deem "not normal".
- That healthy body you long for, but just isn't anymore (or never was).
- The scars you carry from cutting yourself, or the ones from someone else's hand.
- The invisible scars no one sees.
- The mess you've created of your life and can't see a way out of.
- Your prodigal is slumming in all kinds of sordid and treacherous areas.

You name your significant loss. This loss is of great value to you and to our God. What you've lost has created a void, a hole, a vacuum. The question remains, how will you fill the void?

How have you been filling the void (healthy or unhealthy)? If unhealthy, how can you fill it in a better way? Are you willing to see how good and healthy things can become unhealthy when overused to fill the voids?

_____

_____

_____

Will you, have you, been able to cry for your loss? If you haven't, then go ahead and give yourself permission now to cry over what was so very dear to you. Is the shedding of tears difficult for you to let flow? Maybe you feel the need to hold on and control? Please understand that the flow of tears is God given, as well as being healthy for us! Scripture tell us that the Lord collects each tear in one of His bottles (Psalm 56:8). I love that the Living God wanted that recorded in the Bible! He felt it was that important for us to know! When each of us has been emptied of words, tears will speak their own language.

When you can, speak your "feelings", not only your thoughts. Feelings cannot be debated. They come and they go. You don't have to "justify" your feelings. They just are. Feel the feeling because they are God-given, but learn to not be controlled by them.

While others may not think your loss is of great importance (enough for you to truly grieve over) like so many often think of about a miscarriage), this is YOUR loss and not theirs. The void is big, and deep. The Lord Himself will enter and fill all parts with Himself, even to overflowing.

Above all…..Pray to the One who knows you best.

Chapter Five

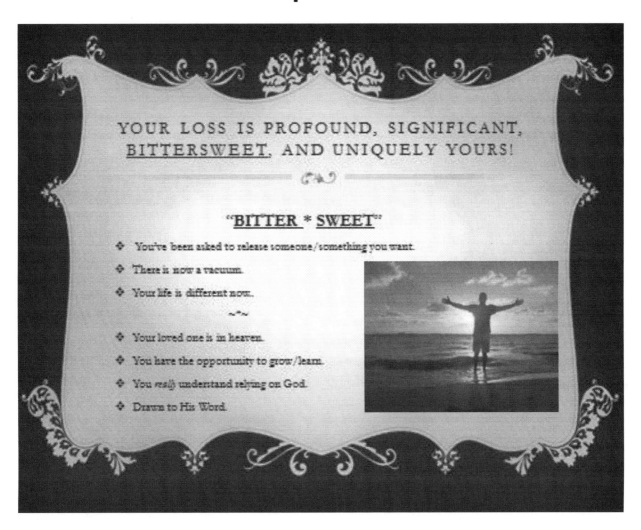

YOUR LOSS IS PROFOUND, SIGNIFICANT, <u>BITTERSWEET</u>, AND UNIQUELY YOURS!

"<u>BITTER * SWEET</u>"

- ❖ You've been asked to release someone/something you want.
- ❖ There is now a vacuum.
- ❖ Your life is different now.

~*~

- ❖ Your loved one is in heaven.
- ❖ You have the opportunity to grow/learn.
- ❖ You *really* understand relying on God.
- ❖ Drawn to His Word.

Bitter/Sweet and Unique

Why bitter? Well, you've been asked to let something go. Naturally you will miss him/her/them or it. Now you must say goodbye, in a million different ways. Each goodbye will feel like a little death; one little death after another. The bitter taste comes because it's a rough reality when every joyous event stirs our memory and we privately have to grieve all over again that which is gone.

> Ephesians 4:23 "...and be renewed in the spirit of your mind, ..."

Ephesians 4:23 is vitally important for everyone. But for those who have abuse in their background, and specifically from their childhood, this is exceedingly crucial. One of the action steps for healing is the pursuit of reprograming/renewing our mind with God's Word. It is so common to have been beaten down with viscous lies from the perpetrator that those lies begin to sink into every cell of our being. Only the Holy Spirit can heal us from the distortions. Even healing the way we might have become 'people pleasers' to pacify those around us; desiring to keep the peace and not make waves. But even in that, the truth is tainted because true love confronts.

If you are the 1 in 3 statistic, having come out of an abusive background (another compound loss comes from damaged emotions), it will be a bit slower and harder for you to move forward than you might realize. There are inappropriate life patterns that have developed and damaged emotions to deal with as well as the loss itself. In order to avoid being a continual victim of the abuse, it may be time to confront (and, yes, even repent of) from the choices used to distract, detach or deadened the soul.

In our past, we have felt the need to protect ourselves, thinking God wasn't capable enough to do it for us or safe enough to trust. In doing so, we have learned certain misbehaviors to handle what we have deemed the impossible. But now is the time to trust, to grow, and to feel the pain of vulnerability so the Lord can touch and heal those places of destruction.

Let's pause to see the difference between unhealthy guilt and having a healthy conviction (where we separate our misplaced behavior from how God truly sees us).

- **Guilt** gives us feelings of being condemned before God and in turn we want to separate ourselves from Him.
- **Conviction** is used by the Holy Spirit to draw us closer to the Lord knowing what we *did* in wrongly dealing in situations might have been unworthy as a child of God, but in that truth we are inspired to repentance.

- **Guilt** leads us in a path of depression, self-pity, fear, sin, bitterness and pride.
- **Conviction** leads us to God in humility, repentance and forgiveness.

💡 Is it helpful to see the difference of Guilt vs Conviction? In what way? Have you ever given these differences some thought?

_____

_____

_____

💡 Do you see any distortion in your thinking between the two?

_____

_____

_____

Why sweet in the Bittersweet?

There is nothing that will uplift our spirit and journey on this earth more than to be become more heavenly minded. Death, loss, and pain will loosen your grip on earthly matters and make you look up towards to the heavens as you call out to Jesus. God draws us to Himself, revealing His heart and desire for those who thirst for more of Him. Understanding the difficult events we face and have to endure are what prepare us for being used on this earth to make a difference.

The world watches as we walk through the fire and they see our devotion to and desperation for God. Our hunger and love of His Word to comfort, direct, and guide us is so evident to those observing. It's a powerful message as others look on and glimpse what 'real' faith looks like! Life becomes sweeter because our prayer life is now richer and our commitment to impart charity and benevolence go deeper in the spiritual realm. As new life patterns change we develop new strengths that lead us to work in His undeniable power.

When trusting in the fullness of God's blessings, think of what you've lost. Compare it to eternity. Try to fuse THAT truth into your thoughts and into your heart. Let it ruminate through you.

💡 Is it helpful for you to know this pain is temporary? In what way? When thinking on eternity does it help you to endure the pain a bit better?

_____

_____

_____

💡 If not right now, can you at least pray that it might help in the future?

_____

_____

_____

Heavenly minded thinking goes like this: Lost a home? You will be given a heavenly mansion not made with human hands. Your health has deteriorated? You will receive a new, incorruptible body fit for heaven (promises we are given throughout the scriptures of the Holy Bible). Lost a loved one? There is a cloud of witnesses waiting to welcome each of us into the biggest family ever. God will make it right. He makes it *all* right. It's His job. He perpetually completes the work in us and restores the losses, always and forevermore. Amen?

"Uniquely Yours"

EVERY circumstance is different and every person's experience is different. So, please do not compare. It is not only cruel, it is wrong to do so. None of us has any idea of what another person has had to endure in their life. No one can fully understand their coping skills. We don't have a clue what might have been unearthed from their past or what they might be dealing with in this most recent loss.

Also, don't judge how another person might be handling their grief, whether it appears good or bad to you. None of us can possibly know what is going on behind closed doors. Maybe they look like they are doing great because they haven't really gone to that hard place yet of working on their grief. It could be that they are wearing the mask of "I'm okay." in order to avoid difficult questions/comments. We just don't know, and should not assume.

It is so important to give extra grace, wiggle room, and time for people to wrestle through their heavy load. Be patient and hold yourself back if you tend to be a natural born "fixer". Remember, their loss cannot be fixed.

Don't rush through the process. God's timing will always be personally and uniquely yours. He works on healing the deepest of places; those we may not even be aware of. Trust His work!! Open yourself up to Him. He is transforming something uniquely for you!!!! God's perspective often is different and grander than most of us can comprehend. It could be a new advocacy, leadership, or ministry opportunity - something that He has called on only you to accomplish. There will be new discoveries, unveilings, and new strengths to share.

There should always be balance, even in grief. Although your suffering is unique to you, it is not unique to mankind.

What is God developing within you? Who are you becoming through this trial? Will you dare to look within and believe that He is developing something new in you?

_____

_____

_____

As the layers begin to unfold (like an onion), and you start to know yourself better, are you becoming all you are meant to be? Can you be excited for the changes, the new ways God is growing you?

_____

_____

_____

Just remember, emotions are here to work for us and not against us.

Above all.....Pray to the One who knows you best.

Chapter 6

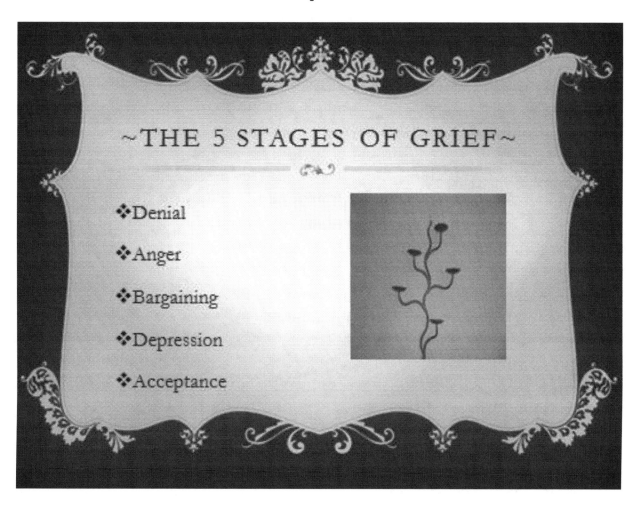

~THE 5 STAGES OF GRIEF~

❖ Denial

❖ Anger

❖ Bargaining

❖ Depression

❖ Acceptance

The 5 Stages of Grief

The commonly known theory "five emotional stages of grief" was first introduced by Elisabeth Kübler-Ross in her 1969 book, *On Death and Dying*.

The 5 stages of grief are:

- **Denial:** Shocked by the initial impact of the realization of the loss confusion sets in. Our natural defense mechanism tells us that this can't be happening! We find that God's kindness covers us during this first part of shock. Shock absorbs the impact of dealing with the traumatic news by allowing our bodies, emotions, and minds to be put on hold for a time during the early stage of grief.
- Moving past the denial stage then brings every other stage of grief into the reality of the loss; which then reveals a deeper and more painful reality.
- **Anger:** Resentment filters in. You begin to play the blame game. You think what has happened is not fair! Often God becomes the target of anger during this stage. It is much easier to redirect our pain and put it on another rather than honestly dealing with our deep ache.
- **Bargaining:** You find yourself wheeling and dealing with God. If He would only do "this" then you would do "that".
- **Depression:** Disconnecting from people and from your spiritual needs. With the reality of the loss hitting so hard you wonder, "Why go on?" In this stage our perceptions are often distorted. There also can be the added component of survivor guilt.
- **Acceptance:** At this point in the journey you are able to come to terms with your reality and start reinvesting in life and with others. You realize you will be okay. It is in this stage that we learn to change our relationship with what we have lost. Though that is hard to hear, and do, it has to happen in order to progress.

Each stage of grief evolves, in time and length. These stages are not sequential and you may not go through one of the stages or you might revisit several of them. This is normal and is more likely plausible. Don't force or avoid any of these stages. Let them come naturally.

Stay close to Jesus. He will let you know if and/ or when you are out of balance in any stage. We have been given the Holy Spirit. It is His job to guide us into truth and help each of us individually. I mention individually because grief is NOT a one size fits all process!

We can't define or dictate how the grief experience will look. Each person is uniquely made. Grief will not fit in some neat and tidy box tied up with a bow. Grief, the normal response to loss, is messy.

💡 Looking back at these different stages of grief, do you recognize yourself in any of the stages? Have you been surprised by any of them? Does one seem more challenging than another?

_____

_____

_____

💡 Are you uncomfortable learning a different side of yourself? Perhaps being surprised by the anger you feel?

_____

_____

_____

Obstacles and Triggers That Can Sabotage Healing

Obstacles to healing can be varied depending on the compound losses suffered. Depending on the frequency of your losses, and those that may still be unresolved, you may discover that you are overloaded and your coping skills are taxed and compromised. You must go back to each loss individually. Identify each one as a loss so you can then work through it. Take your time.

Obstacles develop when we perpetually stay in the "what if's" and the "why's". This freezes our emotions to the event/person; it's as if time has stopped. Self-pity will always block recovery. Stay away from "would have, should have, could have" thinking. It isn't helpful.

Here are a few reactions that can be obstacles in our healing. You might think of them as defensive ways to cope.

- **Rationalization** (minimizing): Comments like, "Oh well, it is what it is." or "I lost one child, but I have two others." only serve to downplay and lessen the pain of the loss. This is done to numb our feelings or to make our grief more palpable to others, so as to protect them or so that they will not be uncomfortable. Real restoration comes when we fully face our pain. It is then that God enters in with His restoring, refreshing remedy.
- **Idealization:** We often take the memory of someone we lost and turn them into a superhuman with no flaws. Or we think the relationship was perfect, as if this honors the dead. It doesn't.
- **Denial:** Avoiding real life by numbing with activities (i.e., turning to food, T.V., computer, social media, gambling, alcohol, drugs etc.). This can be any outside source we turn to instead of looking at God's way of healing our pain.
- **Mathematical Thinker**: A + B always = C. When life does not "add up" we can find ourselves mad at God. You might be blaming someone or something, but ultimately its God your blame truly falls on. You may say, "I'm an American (Republican/tax payer/church tithing Christian, etc.) so this kind of trouble should not come my way!" Not only is this false thinking, and a misunderstanding of the scriptures, it will turn a heart bitter. Life is not a formula to follow.
- **Isolation:** Staying home more than you have before because it's easier than dealing with people's looks and questions. Or perhaps it's just too exhausting because everything reminds you of your loss. Home is a comfort but I would also point out that God needs us. He has a calling on each one of us. If you think someone may be isolating encourage them with that truth.

- **Runner:** People with a background of abuse often do this. You stay busy, busy, busy, as if you are living on a merry-go-round. If you stopped for any length of time it would mean you would have to face your truth. Or, if you stopped long enough, someone might see the truth in you (what you perceive as your truth). So, you hide by staying busy. You may find an obsession for perfection; which, by the way, is unachievable and can even be debilitating to your existence. I am not talking about striving for excellence here but pointing out someone who may have a disproportionate hunger for perfection and control.
- **Digging Your Heels In**: By choosing to be adamant and staying in a self-willed, stuck attitude blocks and eventually destroys your relationship with God. God has asked each of us to keep a teachable heart. Remember the question in scripture when Jesus asked the man at the pool of Bethesda, "Do you want to get better?" (John 5:6). If you get stuck in only being able to see black and white, good or bad, and never see the in-between world, you are missing so much.

Being single and living alone can be an additional obstacle, where moving out of grief can have its own particular challenges. If you are isolating it can be a lonely battle because there is no partner to help cheer you on or hold you on those difficult days. You will need to map out ahead of time what resource to use to reach out to people you can trust and rely on for help. Finding a suitable support group is helpful too. Grief can be so intense at times that you simply cannot expect to rely on only one person to help. God alone can take that grief from us. He never gets exhausted or tired!

There is a lot of beauty to uncover in processing our grief. If you can, picture a prism for a moment. A bright light shines into and through the prism against a black background. What happens? You will see the brilliant colors of the rainbow! It isn't the prism that has changed the colors; it's the light shining through it. Jesus is our Light. We are the prism. The black background might be your past, your difficult memories, the broken world we live in, the anger you carry, the black and white thinking, etc. Uncover the beauty. See the rainbow of colors around you. Let HIS light shine through you and everything else. At some point in time we must ask ourselves, "Do I truly want to get better?" Do you?

As a child of God, we have been brought from death to life by the power of the resurrection through Jesus. In John 11 (verses 43-44) Jesus performs a miracle by raising Lazarus after four days of him being dead and buried. With just three spoken words, "Lazarus, come forth!" Jesus brings him back to life. He then tells the people to remove Lazarus' grave clothes so that he can start living an abundant life!

Is it your time to remove the grave clothes?

_____

_____

_____

💡 Does it frighten you to even think about removing the grave clothes (like Christ told Lazarus to do) because you will feel vulnerable without them? Is there a trusted person in your life that can help you remove the grave wrappings? If you feel 'naked' before our God remember that as a true Christian you are robed in the cloak of the righteousness of Christ in your Father's eyes.

_____

_____

_____

💡 Are you willing to face your pain; face the way you've been coping? Will you use the proper tools to move forward? Is God speaking in these areas for you right now?

_____

_____

_____

Here are a few other kinds of grief to look at that can also be obstacles to healing:
- **Repressed Grief**: When a person hasn't dealt fully with their grief (i.e., refuses those turning points of healing) and creates their own feigned obstacle to heal. This can led to becoming that "sick person" all the time. Repressed grief makes your body, mind, and spirit sick.
- **Abbreviated Grief**: When a spouse dies and the remaining person remarries too soon. You need time to fully grieve. If you don't, then you just bring your junk over into the new marriage.
- **People Pleaser**: When a person is trying constantly to please others in order to keep the peace, not make waves, or keep the world around them in perfect order but in an unbalanced way. Harmony is definitely something to strive for but it also can be unhealthy if you don't stand for truth.

TRUAMA

Let's briefly cover trauma as it pertains to obstacles and to the many losses we face in life. Trauma is being in a continual state of crisis; when abnormal events overwhelm your ability to adapt to life in a healthy way.

Trauma produces a wounding of the brain/spirit/emotions. It takes a toll. Trauma is a thief and an intrusion. If it occurs as a child, then it can hardwire the experience into that child's brain. There can be damage to the brain in the way you process the trauma.

At the moment of trauma the situation renders you powerless. It threatens you. You fear death, or injury of any kind. The horror shatters the belief and assumption that your world is still safe. It changes your beliefs and sense of security. It can produce explosive anger. You must learn to take that energy and put it into long term goals instead of using it up on short term emotions.

Trauma causes hyper alertness. You become hyper vigilant, constantly on guard. Or the opposite, you start to shut down (spiritually, physically, and emotionally). You may feel irritable and jumpy; find it hard to sleep or concentrate because your brain is in the hyper arousal mode. The amygdala is the part of your brain that is your internal alarm; a part that may not be shutting off properly. In trauma you may experience lack of sleep, eating or feel oversensitive.

To understand what happens in trauma, it is now known that 70% of brain bound oxygen is diverted into muscles in order to propel you somewhere else, away from the trauma. So a person in trauma isn't thinking efficiently. They are in a fight, flight, and freeze reaction mode.

The trauma we live in, and through (there is healing), does not mean weakness or some kind of inherited inferiority. Protect yourself from the second wounding that can be done by others who might discount or stigmatize you. Remember, they may have never been confronted by tragedy and cannot fully understand what you are going through. This is applicable for us as well when encountering someone who is dealing with trauma.

The intensity and duration of trauma, whether full or partial, can be a real shock. Be mindful of whether you begin compulsive activities and/or behaviors. Also, look for the beginning of ongoing negative moods, trouble maintaining relationships, or cynical, critical attitudes. If you've been living in a type of "emergency" state for a long time, your adrenal glands might be damaged due to overuse which can lead to not being able to handle smaller stressors in life. If you feel overwhelmed by grief I suggest that it might be time to consult your doctor.

PTSD (Post Traumatic Stress Disorder). Again, this is a normal reaction to abnormal stress, which if severe enough, can alter a person's thinking, feelings, and physical reactions. In trauma, the hippocampus part of the brain is reduced, so that your memory is affected. There is a real chemical reaction going on which affects your brain, which in turn affects your thinking.

All of this can lead to depression, isolation, substance abuse, fear (fear that the loss will repeat), and a sense of doom. Some fear is healthy and needed to make wise choices, but when it becomes unbalanced fear can easily turn into genuine phobias.

It is good to understand your scars and to know your limitations. Respect them. Yet still trust that the Lord can move you forward and build a new history in your brain. This is how you hold onto hope. Your choice is not to live anymore with victim thinking. It no longer serves you because you have been made for more!

Also, trauma rates will be higher coming from an abusive background. The broad definition of abuse is basically any kind of physical, verbal, or emotional cruelty toward a person. Rape is defined by Wikipedia.com as a "type of sexual assault usually involving sexual intercourse or other forms of sexual penetration perpetrated against a person without that person's consent."

Take a moment. Breathe. This information is difficult to go through. It is even more difficult to live though. But have heart! The Lord is your Comforter. He will be with you every step you take. Go slowly, methodically. Give your brain time to adjust. Learn about yourself and learn about your triggers. Triggers are the things that set off emotions related to the trauma.

Triggers: (memories, conscious or unconscious, that set you off)
- Holidays can be not only difficult but can cause triggers. Try to prepare beforehand and be gentle with yourself. You do not have to do all the activities you've done on other holidays.
- Smells can make you react.
- Songs will stir buried emotions.
- Anniversary dates of the loss are big triggers.
- Movies (T.V. in general). Scenes in a movie can jog memories.
- Facebook or social media.
- The sound of an ambulance, fire truck, police car siren.

The list goes on and on.

To get a better understanding of your triggers, start writing them in a journal (who, what, when, where and why). This is a useful tool to help you move forward. To learn what your triggers are enables you to anticipate and to be better prepared to handle them. Relaxed breathing techniques are beneficial in calming down during trigger times. You can check the internet for relaxed breathing techniques to learn and practice.

One such technique, called the **4-7-8 Exercise**:
- Exhale completely through your mouth, making a whooshing sound.
- With your mouth closed, inhale through your nose to the mental count of **four**.
- Hold your breath to the count of **seven**.
- Exhale completely through your mouth making the whooshing sound while mentally counting to **eight**. (Repeat the steps a 2-3 times.)

There may be many triggers that you are simply unaware of, and may never come to know. However, the brain never forgets your history; it's lodged there. You can do your best to understand the when and why's so you can speak God's truth into your reactions. The Lord KNOWS you down to the core of your being. And He loves you completely!

Some ongoing, changing statistics:
- 1 in 4 have been sexually abused (experts now believe it is more like 1 in 3).
- 1 in 4 at some time in life will experience a mental disorder (experts now believe it is more like 1 in 3).
- There is a suicide every 12 minutes in the USA. Interestingly, more suicides happen on a Monday and in the spring. Worldwide, according to National Crime Records Bureau (NCRB), there is one suicide every four minutes (http://www.thehealthsite.com/news/world-suicide-prevention-day-one-suicide-happens-every-four-minutes-according-to-statistics/).

Practical ways to out think the default mode of your suicidal thoughts and start a new groove in the brain with new habits of thinking:
- Breathe deeply. Learn some breathing techniques now *before* you are in a crisis.
- Pray. Ask God to give you the strength to not have damaging thoughts.
- Think about the groove in your brain, and how suicidal/negative thoughts continue along that path and can even make the path larger. Replace the old path with a new groove of positive thoughts and. Fill yourself with God's Word. Know you are His beloved child. Keep special verses nearby to read and reread.
- Do a simple task to distract you and get your thoughts onto something else. This could be as simple as doing the dishes, exercising, writing in a journal, eating, reading, calling a safe friend, etc.
- Ask God to show you what is true; what is the true feeling behind your suicidal thinking. Tell your brain to "take a hike" and that you choose to live! It's a battle for your life!
- Remember, remember, remember...feelings change! You won't always feel this badly.

Now make a copy of these 6 points and put them on sticky notes. Then place them EVERYWHERE!

http://www.suicidepreventionlifeline.org/
Suicide Hotline: 1-800-273-8255

Above all . . . Pray to the One who knows you best.

Chapter Seven

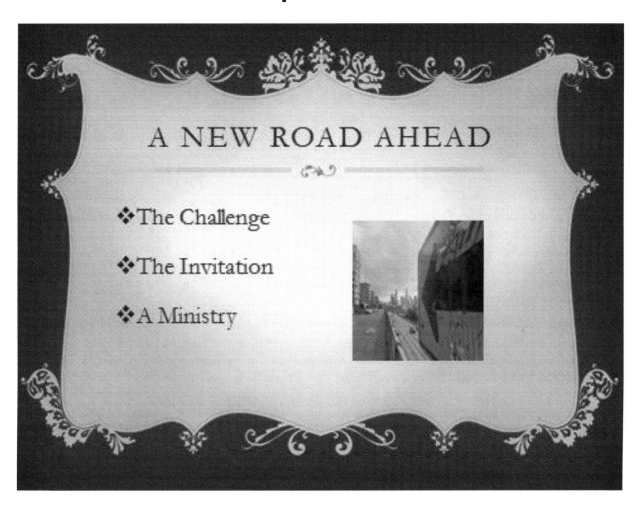

New Road - New Space

This is the final chapter. Basically all the chapters have led up to this last one. It is your ultimate challenge. It is also an invitation to choose healing. Will you gather all that you have learned, grasp that baton, and move forward? Put your newfound knowledge into action in reaching the hurting world around you; one person at a time. Because being in the valley has taught you things.

Yes, everyone would like their time spent in the valley to be brief and thorough, but you may have to visit the valley again. Now when you go there instead of praying *"to get out of it"*, ask God to sustain you in it; to glean all that He will teach you there. In retrospect you have discovered valuable benefits that one day you may even call "a gift"; what you have learned about yourself, about God, and the world around you.

This is a short chapter but it is packed full of lifetime skills that you can choose to embrace and infuse into your future. Make this your prayer - to choose to continue on the healing path, to be more conscious and aware of how you can come along side others whom also desire to heal.

Some of these action tasks are tools I have already mentioned, but every one of us needs a good reminder! Don't worry about timetables when it comes to healing. This is your time. God will give you the grace, wisdom and strength needed to guide you along in the process.

Be in the habit of worship. It is much harder to learn this habit when you find yourself in valley times. Start off slowly. Write yourself sticky notes of praise and thanksgiving to place around the house, or on the monitor of your computer. Take a break in your day to lift up a prayer of thanksgiving and praise to The One who created you.

Move from the 'why' to 'how'. Ask yourself, "Now that this has come into my life, HOW do I work through it?" Open your tightly held fist (which represents a hardened heart) into a budding and thriving open palm. Ask the Lord, "How do I give you glory from this situation?" Be honest with how hard it is for you and that you don't know how you could ever give Him praise in the midst of grief. He is there for you and will demonstrate in your life that cycles can be broken. We can all learn new coping mechanisms and begin a new history for ourselves.

Learn as much as you can about depression, mental illness, God's Word etc. Knowledge is power. Also glean from others who might be on a similar road but just a bit ahead of you. Have them share their wisdom with you.

Forgiveness is vital to healing. Though you may find it difficult (maybe even outrageous to even suggest it), if you choose not to forgive others it will become the stumbling block to healing. You will have to work that out and make peace with it. Sometimes to abide in God means to actively be obedient, even when we don't feel like it. Obedience does not always give off warm fuzzy feelings initially, but it does give great joy ultimately.

Repentance. Oh how we can have a blind spot to our own need for repentance! We may not even be aware that we need to repent. As with forgiveness, repentance is another key element for opening the heart to healing. One cannot, and should not, ever take scissors to the words in the Bible (i.e., forgiveness and repentance) by cutting away subjects that may be uncomfortable or difficult to do. Brokenness over our sin ultimately brings intimate fellowship with God. Scripture says, "Search me, oh God, and know my heart; try me, and know my anxious thoughts; and see if there is any hurtful way in me, and lead me in the everlasting way." (Psalm 139:23-24). Pray for courage to face the mirror.

Transitioning to your new life can be scary facing the unknown tasks ahead, but we can ask for God's help to take our fears and turn them into a mindset of curiosity, as well as expectation. I realize typing these words that it may seem like a simple task but putting them to action is more challenging. It is possible though, with God by our side. I believe in hope!

Preparation is another key tool. Find new ways to function without *whom* or *what* you have lost. This might mean having to change some of your activities (either add to or let go of). You may be struggling with this new identity. The "we" turning into the "I" is NOT an easy transition to make!!!! Always remember, your identity comes from Christ, and Christ alone. You are His workmanship, His child; chosen, holy and blameless; His friend, a fellow heir. He loves you perfectly and unconditionally. As you prepare for this 'new' normal, decide what to keep and what to let go of. Even Jesus helped his mom transition by preparing her to take John as a son and asking John to take His mother as his own; a beautiful example for us.

I believe there is great benefit in doing a Graph Journal. This is where you draw a line and mark a time period in your life when there were difficulties; as well as the easy, fun times. Mark the emotions you felt. It is a good visual of seeing patterns, strengths, and times your anger arose, when you cried the most, times you were the loneliest, etc. Example:

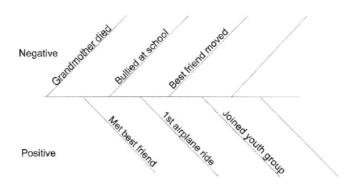

Keep the graph and when some time has passed do another one and compare the two. Also, these are very helpful in understanding your triggers (what songs make you cry or what noises bring the fear/anxiety back). No worries if you don't feel you have moved very far forward. The first graph serves as a baseline. Trust that you will keep operating from the position of strength because you are now staying close to God and He is your helper. Seeing your truth on paper helps you visually work to keep your emotions more balanced.

> Isaiah 61:1 *"The Spirit of the Lord GOD is upon me, because the LORD has anointed me to bring good news to the afflicted; He has sent me to bind up the brokenhearted, to proclaim liberty to captives and freedom to prisoners"*

Often when we read above verse, we think of how our Lord came to give the Good News and hope to unbelievers of His time. And this of course is correct. But, He is also speaking to those who call Him Lord and have a personal relationship with Him today. When our emotions are entangled with grief and we begin to wonder if it will always be like this, the answer is an emphatic NO! When we begin to admit our need (poor in spirit), when we surrender our broken heart to Him, healing begins. He has promised freedom from the dark prison cell we have erected around ourselves. The key awaits us to take hold of it. Hope is a certainty in our future in Him. He then becomes The Light (The Light is always with us) in whatever darkness we find ourselves in at the moment. Our job is to believe that truth.

If you get to understand your grief better you will move through it in a fuller, more honest way. Again, then you can assist others to execute their own healing honestly and fully.

More tangible ways to heal:

- Keep a journal. Journaling helps sift through the emotions of grief. It clears the mind and relieves pent up pressure. Write letters to those alive or to those who have passed on. It's freeing to regurgitate past hurts and emotions that are holding you back. No one needs to see the letter. It's therapeutic to just go through the process. If you don't like to write, then try drawing your pain or enjoy some musical therapy.
- Give a charitable contribution in someone's name so their memory will live on.
- Perform a symbolic act of erecting an 'Ebenezer Stone'; Ebenezer means "the stone of help". Basically it's a stone memorial of where God has met you as well as an acknowledgement that He has brought (or is bringing) you through a battle. We read in the First Book of Samuel how the Israelite's did this when the Palestinians were defeated and victory was theirs. It was tangible reminder for them of God's Holy Presence, His aid, and also as a marker to others of His great help.
- Think of life as a mosaic piece of art; the beauty that a mosaic represents. Broken pieces intentionally lain out (not hidden), intertwined, intersecting, infused, and lining up to form a whole piece. Woven together in a beautiful, honest piece of work. We too should live out our life as a mosaic, showing what broken pieces God has merged together in His expert craftsmanship.

Tangible ways to help others move through loss or trauma:

- Reassure them *in* Christ, being careful to not give a cliché, or false assurances. Don't promise what you cannot deliver.
- Ask the person how they might feel more supported. They may not know at the time, but it does get them thinking.
- There is a "wet cement" theory when it comes to trauma. Getting help within the first 24-hours lessens the imprint trauma has on someone.
- Give HOPE. Always! Speak in soft tones, keep it simple. Remember what has happened to this person's brain and the possibility that they're in shock. We must never forget the power the Holy Spirit and our calmness can bring to a hurting individual. Most of us feel inadequate in what to say or if we should say anything. Just our presence sitting alongside them in the mess speaks volumes. Don't worry about what to say. Trust that the Lord will give you the compassionate words you need when you need them.
- Learn to listen with your heart. Hear their story. You really don't need to talk or advise. Just listen. Look for verbal and nonverbal language to truly know how they are doing. Clarify what was said and then repeat it back to them.
- Don't try to fix them. You can't. Only the Holy Spirit can do that. You don't have to be their cheerleader either.

- Be careful not to rush them or use clever words. Just keep encouraging them in the LORD, with no judgment. At some point you may need to confront any discrepancy between reality in how they perceive their situation or in their behavior, but now may not be that time. Also, in a crisis, whatever normal behavioral tendencies people have will emerge and be even more robust than usual, so expect them to behave differently.
- Help them to operate from a position of strength. You might need to re-label what has happened to help them see their situation in a more positive light. Be careful! You always want to validate what has happened and how they feel at the present time.
- People need to be nurtured and know they have been heard and understood. But most of all they need to feel accepted. Enter their world and adapt to their needs at that moment.
- Allow for silence. Don't be uncomfortable just sitting in silence. They are trying to process so many things about what has happened. Be attentive and be patient.
- If they've lost is a loved one, ask what the deceased's name is if you didn't know them. Then use it in conversation. Don't be afraid of that. In fact, it is like music to their soul to hear their loved one's name.
- Anticipate triggers. Help them through them. Watch for any dangerous behavior.
- Children come in and out of grief. That is why they can go out and play and seem to act like nothing has happened one minute and then be out of control the next. Make sure to allow for that. It might also be harder for them to verbalize their pain. Help them speak their pain through artwork.
- Sometimes your faith will have to carry your friend or loved one until theirs returns. *"Help carry each other's burdens. In this way you will follow Christ's teachings." Galatians 6:2*

As this workbook comes to an end, it is really just the beginning of your journey of healing. Revisit it every so often to remind yourself of what you have learned and to see your progress. There is always something more to glean as time goes by; a little nugget you may not have seen, or understood at the time you first did the work.

I believe in your healing because I believe in Whom all healing comes from. Be blessed in our Lord Jesus Christ.

Above all . . . Pray to the One who knows you best.

Other Contacts:

Griefshare: http://www.griefshare.org

N.A.M.I. (National Alliance on Mental Illness): https://www.nami.org

Suicide Prevention Lifeline: http://www.suicidepreventionlifeline.org/

Suicide Hotline: 1-800-273-8255

Above all . . . Pray to the One who knows you best.

About The Author

- Kerry Monroe lives in the state of Washington.
- She's a widow and mother of three grown children.
- Survivor.
- Author of God Always Knew. Founder of **A.N.E.W**. Grief Care and Coaching (**A**cknowledge/**N**avigate/**E**ducate/**W**illingness)
- Facilitator for the Suicide Support Group in Whatcom County Washington
- Part-time Chaplain for RailRoad Chaplains USA
- Part-time Chaplain for MarketPlace USA
- Certified by Norman Wright Grief Coaching Center
- Certified by N.A.M.I. Family to Family (**N**ational **A**lliance on **M**ental **H**ealth)
- Certified by Billy Graham's Rapid Response Training
- Bible Study leader
- Previously on Children's Hospital Parental Advisory Cancer Board
- Previously Women's Ministry Director, Sunday school teacher, Awana's Director
- A fellow wounded warrior in God's Army.

IN CHRIST, WE ARE...

DELIVERED FROM DEATH –
RENEWED AFTER REDEMPTION –
MOVED OVER MERCY –
TRANSFORMED THROUGH THRUTH –
STRENGTHENED HAVING SUFFERED –
FACED WITH FORGIVENESS –
CALLED FOR COMPASSION –
GUIDED TOWARDS GRACE –
FREED IN FAITH –
HELD BY HOPE –
AND LIBERATED TO LOVE.
~~*~~

Simple Blessings,
KM